PSALMS AND OTHER SONGS
FROM A PIERCED HEART

Psalms and Other Songs from a Pierced Heart

Patricia Stevenson, RSJ

With a Foreword by Alice Camille

LITURGICAL PRESS
Collegeville, Minnesota

www.litpress.org

Cover design by Monica Bokinskie. Photo courtesy of Getty Images.

First published 2003. New and enlarged edition 2012.

© 2012 Patricia E. Stevenson, RSJ, Sisters of St. Joseph of the Sacred Heart, 56 Selwyn Avenue, Mission Bay, Auckland.

© 2019 by Patricia Stevenson, RSJ

1	2	3	4	5	6	7	8	9

Library of Congress Cataloging-in-Publication Data

Names: Stevenson, Patricia, RSJ, author. | Camille, Alice L., writer of foreword.
Title: Psalms and other songs from a pierced heart / Patricia Stevenson ; with a foreword by Alice Camille.
Description: Collegeville, Minnesota : Liturgical Press, [2019] | "First published 2003. New and enlarged edition 2012"—Title verso. | Summary: "A retelling of psalms and other familiar Scripture texts reminding readers of the communion that unites the joys and sufferings of people everywhere"—Provided by publisher.
Identifiers: LCCN 2019021823 (print) | LCCN 2019980895 (ebook) | ISBN 9780814664629 (paperback) | ISBN 9780814664865 (ebook)
Subjects: LCSH: Bible. Psalms—Paraphrases, English.
Classification: LCC BS1440 .S85 2019 (print) | LCC BS1440 (ebook) | DDC 223/.206—dc23
LC record available at https://lccn.loc.gov/2019021823
LC ebook record available at https://lccn.loc.gov/2019980895

This book is for all people who love the Scriptures and know they are a well that never runs dry.

My thanks to all those who have joined with me over the years, my family, friends, fellow explorers and teachers.

Contents

Foreword

I've not met Patricia Stevenson. Yet in all the ways that matter I feel I have, through her songs from a pierced heart.

This book came to me as a gift from my friend Jennifer, a fellow sister of Patricia's. When it arrived, I glanced ruefully at the bookcase, which already contains nine translations and paraphrases of the Psalms. I was tempted to stack this one with the rest. After all, like a lot of folks, I pray the Liturgy of the Hours daily. My life is stuffed fat with psalms.

Yet Jennifer had sent the book to me. She's an artist and mystic, and I'm always hopeful of seeing the world better through her eyes. So instead of shelving this gift, I decided to read it. What a surprise it turned out to be.

Patricia Stevenson's inspired paraphrase of psalms and other biblical passages reveals why we still look to ancient texts to express fresh ideas. What brings us back to the psalms, again and again, is that these yellowed old prayers are very like our shiny recent attempts at praying. They are the cries of believing hearts—hearts that, like our own, are not always as faithful as we might wish. Psalms hold the world of human experience within their borders: joy, pain, relief, fear, hope, outrage, exultation, despair, wonder, weariness, and more. It's the emotional content of these texts—not their poetry, antiquity, or origins—that draws us to them. So in choosing a translation to ferry our prayers, it's important to find one that taps this passion.

Some may ask: Why reinterpret old texts at all? Aren't the original phrases enough? Think in terms of music and it makes sense. A song is written and recorded, is soon beloved, becomes a classic, and may over time seem immutable. When Pete Seeger composed and sang "Turn! Turn! Turn! (To Everything There Is a Season)," for example, that might have been enough. But who would want to have missed The Byrds' memorable take on this song—or subsequent versions by Judy Collins, Marlene Dietrich, Dolly Parton?

Seeger himself, of course, was adapting an antique set of verses from Ecclesiastes. Turn, turn, turn indeed! Reshaping a good idea is rarely a bad idea. It is, in fact, the soul of homiletics, art, love letters, not to mention every gospel after the first one. So maybe ten translations of psalms on one's shelf are not excessive, but simply a good start.

As T. S. Eliot put it: "Good writers borrow. Great writers steal." Eliot may have stolen this motto from Picasso, who said the same thing about artists. The point being that anything worth creating is worth a good re-vision now and then.

The biblical adaptations here are enchanting because they are well chosen and well said. As a seeker, I love the questions Patricia raises in these prayers: Do you want to be happy? Where does trouble come from? Why does God care for us? These are queries worth pursuing for any believer.

As a writer, I appreciate the clarity, brevity, and honesty of these prayers. The familiar version of Psalm 100, for example, is four verses long. But Patricia distills it down to four pithy lines of text: a miracle of economy, no less powerful for being succinct. Or how about this stunning interpretation from Psalm 33: "God speaks: we have a universe." The story of creation, delivered in six words!

How we might long for world leaders to heed her simple, authoritative directions in the verses inspired by Psalm 72: reduce poverty, protect children, value justice. The poetry sings in lines like "Let us wear your grace as our true clothing" and "When I see the birds / wheeling in the sky, / I wish for wings to rise above the storms" (riffs on Psalms 5 and 55, respectively).

Yet it's the Jewish-flavored chutzpah in these meditations that I value most. Here's a phrase I must have intended to lob upward in prayers past and will surely use in the future, now that I've learned it: "I think my prayer deserves an answer" (from Psalm 17)! Come now, let's be frank: Don't we all feel the same?

I can't think of a more poignant interpretation of Psalm 69's pleading stance than this: "Look at me, when I'm speaking! / I feel desperate." We might say this to a friend or family member. Why not to God?

This is real conversation, delivered by a woman who must have such unadorned talk with the people in her life, including her Maker. Patricia captures the bartering spirit of the psalmist—"I promise to deal with my depression" (from Psalm 43)—and also how that doesn't always pan out in real life: "God, I feel depressed again" (from Psalm 69). Such intimacy between psalmist and interpreter is beyond commentary. It's closer to channeling.

Highlighting my secret favorite phrases in this short introduction is as hopeless as it is unnecessary. There's a line that leaps up to find me on each page; and naturally, you'll discover your own, based on the life you happen to be living. And isn't that the way of Scripture, after all—to meet us where we are?

Patricia doesn't include her personal encounter with all 150 psalms, but she does add explorations of Isaiah's Servant Songs, and passages from Lamentations, Sirach, and Wisdom. Even a few New Testament texts get her special treatment. At first I felt a little cheated of other texts I would have liked to see included. Then it occurred to me that the pierced heart summoned up by the title refers not just to Patricia, or to the original composers of these verses. Each reader who savors holy texts risks a similar piercing. We who pray are invited to make these passages, and the ones that didn't make it into this book, our own. "We, too, must continue the line of storytellers" (from Psalm 105).

Happiness

If you want to be happy:
avoid evil,
choose to make God's word
your delight and guide.
Study it always.

You will be like a fruitful evergreen
on the banks of a stream.

Unwise choices
leave you like litter in the wind,
blown about achieving nothing.
There is only ruin in store for the corrupt.

Let God be your compass.

inspired by Psalm 1

Learn to Serve

Why is there so much trouble in the world?
Why is time wasted
in destructive plotting?

There are those who place personal power above
    everything,
even their own people.

God knows their plans
will achieve no good.
God shares authority with those who are humble;
with those who work
for the good of all.
Come to your senses you who wield power.
Learn to serve the Lord with joy.

inspired by Psalm 2

Trust

Faithful God, hear my prayer.
You have helped me in the past.
When I've felt threatened by darkness I've tried to
    be calm.

When I've felt caught in endless night
I've tried to keep you as my lodestar.

In the face of trouble I hold tight to your word.
Your gifts mean more to me than material things.
My security in the face of the unknown is a loving
    blessing.

inspired by Psalm 4

Help

Hear my words that are heavy with sadness.
My prayer begins with the dawn and in trust I wait.

I try to avoid evil, especially all violence,
as I know it offends the spirit of your kingdom.

Your mercy has given me the strength to pray.
Help me clear my path so that your justice may be
    my light.

Let all believers come together in praise of God.
Let us wear your grace as our true clothing.

inspired by Psalm 5

Wonder

God, creator, the whole world breathes your name.
Your goodness reaches out beyond the stars.

The joyful babble of babies
has the power to move the hardest hearts.
We see your artwork in the gallery of the universe.

To see the stars and planets in their mystery
is to wonder at the littleness of us humans.

You care for us in a special way.
You have called us to stewardship of the earth.
To be cocreators and guardians of the universe
is a lifetime responsibility.
Let us honor your life-giving name.

inspired by Psalm 8

Thanksgiving

With hearts full of thanks
we proclaim what you have done.
You are our joy, O God.
We sing out our praise.
Darkness has no power in your presence.

You act on the side of justice.
False ambition is reduced to rubble.
You are the source of justice.
You teach us to judge rightly.
The oppressed know you as their strength.
The faithful know your abiding presence.

inspired by Psalm 9

Justice

We have made God our shelter.
Like birds in hunting season, we seek safety.
In a life of justice, violence has no place.
Those who choose violence know self-destruction.

God loves justice.
Those who act justly see God.

inspired by Psalm 11

Grief

Lord, keep remembering me.
Why do I feel
that you have turned from me?
Must I grieve forever?
Must I always carry pain?
Do those against me always have to win?

My God, look at me,
let your radiance cover me or I will die.
Do not let my tormentors boast
that they have defeated me.

I trust in you, my love.
I will sing of the Lord
who treats me with kindness.

inspired by Psalm 13

Live Justly

The house of God is open to all.
Those who live with God are known by their
integrity, courageous truth,
and right living.

The just do not slander their neighbors,
or abuse the trust of friends;
neither do they profit from the misfortunes of others.

Their word is their bond.

inspired by Psalm 15

Protector

Protect me, God; you are my help.
I once put material goods and worldly ambition
ahead of your will.
Those pursuits caused me nothing but grief.

Lord, you are all I need.
I give thanks for the lessons you have taught me.
My heart leaps with joy
with your energy in me.
At your side I travel the road of life.

inspired by Psalm 16

Deliver Me

Hear me, God; give me your full attention.
I think my prayer deserves an answer.
You have probed my heart and have seen
    my integrity.
I live your word, avoiding violence.

Keep a loving eye on me.
I appeal to you as my mother.
If a mother bird protects her young,
you will do no less for me.

Sometimes I feel ambushed
by my weaknesses and negative tendencies.
Deliver me from harm.
Let me rise each morning filled with the knowledge
of your presence.

inspired by Psalm 17

My Rock

I love you, God my strength.
You are like a rock at my back.
You keep me safe.

Death held me in its grip.
I felt swept away in a fierce current.

Out of these depths I cried in my fear,
you heard me, my rock.

I give thanks because you anchored me.
You freed me from the clinging weeds of fear,
enabling me to give thanks for your fidelity.

inspired by Psalm 18

God's Creation

The genius of God
is displayed in creation.
Night and day proclaim
the word of God in silence.
The sun appears like an athlete
running a course from east to west.
All on earth know its benefits and fear its power.

God's law is reflected in the order of the universe.
Even the unsophisticated can
understand its demands.
What God asks, delights us with its
dear providence.

God's design for the universe is like
the offer of centered happiness.
Sometimes I have misunderstood
or misused this gift.
Forgive me my clumsiness.

Unmindfulness blocks my appreciation.
Keep me godly in thought and deed.
Your grace supports me.

inspired by Psalm 19

13

Feeling Abandoned

God, I feel abandoned even by you.
I cry in the dark;
my pain seems endless.
I recall the trust placed in you
by people through the ages.
You have brought comfort in the most difficult times.

Fear and pain make me feel that I am nothing.
Others seem to mock me;
they don't see my deep despair.

Yet, I know that you too have mothered me.
In my mother's womb and at her
breast you have watched over me.
This loving closeness I need to feel, now!

inspired by Psalm 22

14

My Shepherd

The Lord is my shepherd.

When I need rest, you give me the fragrant grass.
By burbling streams, my spirit revives.
Along the steep tracks in the hills, my feet are steady.
Should I fall into a gully, your crook will reach me.

The Lord is my host and comforter.

You call me to your table.
You massage my aching head with healing oils.
You feed me royally.

Shepherding goodness
and comforting love,
watch over me every day.
My dwelling with God is my true home.

inspired by Psalm 23

Wondrous

This universe
is a wondrous work of God.
Climb a hill and inhale the landscape.
Stand on the shore and feel the song of the sea.

Are we fit inheritors of this bounty?
Have we enough integrity to recognize
substance from shadow?

Those who seek God will see God.
God's blessing is universal justice.

Open the door of your heart.
Allow creator God to enter.

inspired by Psalm 24

Guide Me

God, I give myself to you;
I do this with trust in your faithfulness.

Teach me how to live.
Show me the right way for me.

God, remember me.
You have guided people through the ages.
It is your goodness that saves.
Forgive me when I miss the mark.

I know that I will have fullness of life
with you as my guide.

inspired by Psalm 25

Trust in God

God is my light, my strong defense.
Why should I fear when storms threaten me?
When problems come at me from all directions,
I will hold firmly to my trust in God.

I would love to live my life
fully aware that,
with the universe,
I am a temple of God.

As a tent pitched on firm ground,
secure and open I live in safety.
I will play and sing like a child.

inspired by Psalm 27

The Voice of God

Spirits of the universe,
give glory to God.
The voice of God is heard in storms,
rousing all creatures.
God's voice strikes fire from desert rocks.
The universe heaves and writhes in labor.

The universe exalts in new birth.
Glory to God!
Strength to your people!

inspired by Psalm 29

Abundant Mercy

I hovered on the brink of despair.
You pulled me back and healed me.

Give thanks, all living things, to this awesome God.
As morning laughter follows
a brief night of tears,
so my fear of God
is lost in abundant mercy.

When all is going well, I feel invincible.
When things go wrong, I forget God
and feel abandoned.
I cry for help; I want it now!
Like a petulant child, I try to threaten God.

The minute I am conscious
of God's saving presence,
it's off with the sackcloth
and on with the glad rags.

And again I promise undying gratitude.

inspired by Psalm 30

Forgiveness

Those who have experienced
forgiveness are happy.

If I try to hide my wrongdoing,
my body suffers.
I feel your judgment
like a heavy hand.
If I face what I have done, the weight lifts.

No wonder the saints teach us
that mercy encircles us
with songs of freedom.

God is our guide on mountain tracks.
If we act like mules, we'll need bridle and bit.
We know that evil has its consequences
and that trust in God brings strength.

We are slow to learn the songs of faithfulness.

inspired by Psalm 32

All-Powerful God

Orchestra and choir show us how to praise God.
With each day we sing a new song to God.
The word of God is a holy deed.
God, lover of truth and justice,
fills the earth with love.

God speaks: we have a universe.
God breathes: stars appear.
Through the action of God all things
come into being.

Blest are the people who acknowledge
God as creator.
God who made our hearts knows our dreams,
hopes, and fears.
Governments proclaim that peace will come through
weapons of war;
we know that such reliance on force is futile.

God cares for those who suffer.
God calls on us to save.
We attend to God's call as faithful servants.

inspired by Psalm 33

22

Give Thanks

I give thanks always.
My praise is constant.
The poor will take heart from God's fidelity.

Join me in this ministry of thankfulness.
I have learned it from experience of God's kindness.
My heart is glad as I drink in the riches of God.
This wine of God's strength sustains me.

inspired by Psalm 34

Be Good

Don't concern yourself with other people's faults.
Be good and be at peace.

Give your life to God.
God will be your advocate.

Let your integrity light up the world.
In stillness ponder the goodness of the Lord.

inspired by Psalm 37

My Sins

Sometimes I fear your justice, God.
Those who are totally at one with God
are conscious of time wasted,
of opportunities lost,
of selfishness.

I feel paralyzed by my inadequacies;
I grieve for my sins and shortcomings.
I know you will not abandon me.
Help me to be whole.

inspired by Psalm 38

25

My Help

I felt bogged down.
I waited for God to help me
out of the swamp of my own dejection.

God has placed me on solid ground.
God has taught me a new song of praise.
Many will be moved by my example.

You did not ask for elaborate rituals,
but you demand new ears.
I promise to live by the Scriptures,
writing your living word in my heart.

inspired by Psalm 40

Voiceless

Blessed are those who work for the voiceless.
God rains blessings on those engaged
in saving work.

Those who work for justice know
the wrath of the unjust.
Even trusted friends don't always understand.
We have to hold fast against popular opinion.
In the face of criticism we seek the comfort of God.

inspired by Psalm 41

Thirst for God

As the timid deer
clings to the shadow of the bush,
craving the bubbling waters,
afraid to venture from safety,
I, too, thirst for God.

Tears have been my steady diet.
I recall the days of my first fervor
when all was joy
in the service of God.

I ask myself, "What has changed?"
Why am I so easily upset by people's
attitudes and opinions?
Prayer is difficult.
I feel sad and grieve for the past.

Then the memory of God's goodness
bubbles up in my heart.
I rise to praise God even in darkness.

inspired by Psalm 42

Help Me

I stand before God to plead my case.
Against me stand those aspects
of myself that threaten
to engulf me.

Help me climb the mountain
of new insight
lit by the twin lamps
of light and truth.

I give praise to God with my being and my talents,
I promise to deal with my depression.

inspired by Psalm 43

Hospitality

My heart bursts with a new song.
Love makes my tongue as skilled as the finest poet.

Because I have espoused justice,
I am anointed with holy oil.

Because I have put on the garments of discipleship,
I feel transformed.

I have put aside the pursuit of vain ambition.
I accept with gratefulness the hospitality of God.

inspired by Psalm 45

In God's Hands

The cosmos teaches us
lessons about God.

When we feel earthquakes
and see the power of volcanoes
or tidal waves that ambush the shore,
we learn that all the earth is in God's hands.

Such natural power calls us to humility.
Our manufactured forces are
a mockery of true creative energy.
God with us is all the power we need.

inspired by Psalm 46

Ovation

We clap our hands
and give a standing ovation to God
who is above all the wonders
and artistry that we can imagine.

Through the ages we have
celebrated the mighty deeds of God
with music, art, and human crafts.

Reflect on your gifts
and then use them for
the glory of God.

inspired by Psalm 47

Praise God

Let all the earth be the city of God!

Let each mountain summon us
to raise our hearts and minds.
Let our praise fill the earth
like the winds that circle the globe.

On every walk be aware of the beauty around you
that you may pass this message on to your children.

Death, the great darkness,
is no match for God's light.

inspired by Psalm 48

Grateful

If God were to put us on trial,
of what would we stand accused?

We worship regularly,
but God did not demand this.

What is the point of worship
if our hearts are not in it;
if it does not change us?

We stand or fall on whether we have
a grateful heart.

inspired by Psalm 50

Healed

Have mercy, gentle God.
Let the waters of your grace
wash over me.

You see me for what I am;
your justice reveals my inadequacies.

You call me to be centered in truth.
For this I need to learn wisdom.

Let me rise from the waters, newborn,
my heart filled with gladness.

Reshape my heart so that I, too,
may teach others your way.

The gift I bring to you is a spirit
once broken,
now healed by your love.

inspired by Psalm 51

Dark Times

I need reassurance that you hear me, God.
In dark times when I feel threatened,
it's hard to live by faith.

When I see the birds
wheeling in the sky,
I wish for wings to rise above the storms.

I see, too, the violence and oppression
that stalk our land unchecked.
It makes me want to hide.

You, ever my friend,
who have been my constant companion,
with whom I have always shared my heart,
I treasure your faithful love.

inspired by Psalm 55

Trust without Fear

God, I need your help.
I feel attacked on all sides.
I tell myself that when I'm afraid I trust in you.
Can these evils really destroy me?

I wish that all evil in the world
could be wiped out.
I've wept enough;
is there no record of my tears?

I hold tight to your promises.
I trust without fear.
I will always walk at your side
in the light of your glory.

inspired by Psalm 56

Threatened

Take pity on me, Lord.
Let me feel the shadow of your presence
hovering over me.

I feel trampled upon
by the difficulties of my life.
Be kind to me, God.
I feel threatened
as if besieged by the malicious.

I will be steadfast; help me, God.
Wake up, my soul!
Night is over, wake the dawn.
I will start my prayers of thanksgiving
even while it is still dark.

Glory to you, God in all the universe.

inspired by Psalm 57

Defenseless

You have broken down my defenses, God.
Help me repair the cracks before I fall apart.
I have experienced hardship and pain
and I feel bewildered.

I need a sanctuary.
I feel as if you have rejected me.
Give me what I need to serve you.

With you to lift me up, I can be valiant.

inspired by Psalm 60

Shelter Me

Hear my prayer, my God.
My spirit is weak.
I seem to be calling
from a long way off.

Mother eagle, shelter me under your wings.
May I find a dwelling place with you forever.

You have accepted my vows.
You have given me the inheritance of the faithful.

I will be faithful to my vows,
renewing them each day.
My life will be a hymn of praise.

inspired by Psalm 61

True Haven

I wait in silence.
God is my savior, rock, refuge, and safety net.

I meditate on what is happening around me.
The way we treat each other
as if others are fences
that can be pulled down;
the charming word that conceals a destructive heart.

I wait in God's silence,
rock, refuge, safety net,
and true haven of hope.

Our lifetime is but a breath.
The only true riches are gifts from God.
Our wages are paid according to our godly deeds.

inspired by Psalm 62

41

Longing

I thirst.

My body aches like the parched earth without rain.
Sleeplessness gives me time to recall your goodness.
I need a vision to call me on.

The Image of the eagle lifting its young comforts me.
I cling to you.

Truth is our constant joy.

inspired by Psalm 63

42

Grateful Pilgrims

From all over the world
we come to you,
like the procession of travelers to a holy shrine.
Everyone knows that they are welcome.

People everywhere stand in awe of your works.
As a good farmer prepares the land for sowing,
you tend your people.

The earth is filled with people
who reveal your fruitfulness through lives of mercy,
kindness, and gratefulness.

This is worth singing about.

inspired by Psalm 65

Tested

Let us join the earth in praising God.
As metals are refined by fire,
so we are tested by our difficulties.

I can now acknowledge your help.
As I passed through fire and water,
I thought I was lost.

I now tell others of your support.
I do this with a grateful heart.
God has always been a constant listener.

inspired by Psalm 66

Comforted

Like wax in flame
and mist before the sun,
so those perish
whose hearts are earthbound.

Sing a litany of godly works.
Parents to the orphan;
comfort to the widowed;
home for the wanderer;
open door for prisoners.

Like the sudden downpour that refreshes,
you bring comfort and strength.

inspired by Psalm 68

Desperation

God, I feel depressed again.
Because I make you my center,
I feel estranged from family and friends.

Passion for your dream takes all my energies.
I tried traditional practices of penance,
but they alienate me from others.

Don't let me drown in the mud of my negativity.
It takes so long to be free of it.

Look at me, when I'm speaking!
I feel desperate.
I'm sick at heart.
I looked around for comfort and sympathy,
but I found nothing.

God hears the poor.
God does not despise my worries.
Praise God!
God creates, God rebuilds.
Great is the company of women who preach
    the gospel.

inspired by Psalm 69

Come to My Aid

Come to my aid, gracious God!
I need your assistance.

I feel threatened on all sides.
Let me not fall into ruin like an abandoned house.

There are some who mock me,
who make fun of my efforts to serve you.

Let them seek you and be glad in you.
Let all cry: God be glorified.

inspired by Psalm 70

My Haven

Lord, you are my shelter.
You are dependable.
You deliver and save.

Be my rock, my haven, my tower of strength.

From my mother's womb,
through my childhood and youth,
you have been a reliable presence.
For this I praise you.

Now that I am getting older,
do not toss me aside as others do.

From childhood you have taught me to praise you.
I still have the energy to teach a new generation
of your boundless goodness.

I thank you, Lord, for your true friendship.
I will make my life a melody of joy.

inspired by Psalm 71

Leadership

God, give our leaders true judgment,
your sense of what is right.
Be with them
as they use their authority
on behalf of the people.

These are the gifts we wish for our leaders:
that they will reduce poverty;
that they will protect children;
that they will value justice;
that they will be a voice for the voiceless;
that they will care for the abandoned;
that they will work for true peace.

inspired by Psalm 72

Envy

I have been envious of those
who have more than I have.
I've envied their confidence,
their good looks, and their success.

I've been stupid, letting envy embitter me.
The best thing I did was stay close to you.
You took my hand and taught me wisdom.

What more could you have given me than yourself?
Who delights in me as much as you do?
I treasure your closeness.

inspired by Psalm 73

50

God's Great Deeds

Listen to me, my people,
take notice of each word.

I'll begin with a story.
I will tell of mysteries
welling up from ancient springs.

These truths have been the treasure of our elders.
These stories are the heritage of our children.

The stories are of God's great deeds
throughout the ages.
Stories of creating, of saving, of teaching, of healing;
stories of trust, of fidelity and commitment.
We will never forget what God has done for us.

inspired by Psalm 78

Like a Vineyard

Good Shepherd, listen to our cries.
We have wandered from the light you offer us.

We have known the bitterness of barren places,
the only springs, our tears.

Once we were like a vineyard,
lush, fruitful, filling the valley from mountain to sea.
Now we are drought-ridden, broken, without hope.

May we again draw our strength from you.
May you be our gentle vintner.

inspired by Psalm 80

Our Memories Were Short

We've sung the song of a freed people.

Once we were brought out of slavery.
God lifted the load from our backs.
God heard the cries of our pain.
God gave us food on the journey.

But our memories were short.
We found new gods.
We left you out of our plans.
We chose our own paths.

You know we lack the ability
to listen with the heart.

Teach us to walk in your ways.

inspired by Psalm 81

My True Home

Your home is my joy.
It's my true dwelling place.

As sparrows home in on food,
as swallows seek a nesting site,
so I seek my true home.

To live with God is joy.
My praise and gratitude
is never-ending.
My life is a journey homeward,
a pilgrimage through the seasons of life.

God blesses those who walk with integrity.

inspired by Psalm 84

Revive Us

Lord, you love your land.
When we experience exile,
you draw us home.

We fear the weakness of our infidelity.
We depend on you for the energy to repent.
Revive us, nourish us, and show us mercy.

I recall your words of peace.
Love and fidelity, peace and justice
are our parents.

The love of God poured out recreates the earth.
Justice is both trailblazer and signpost.

inspired by Psalm 85

Rescue Me

Hear me, God, and do something,
for I am poor and helpless.
I am your loyal servant; rescue me.

Every waking hour I seek your mercy.
I plead in my despair for you to act.

Make your path clearer so that I may follow safely.
Make my one desire to cherish your name.

inspired by Psalm 86

Covenant

I sing songs of your love and faithfulness.

I honor the covenant you made with me.
Our ancestors in the faith knew you were steadfast.
We were taught to see you as our parent.
We were taught to speak to you with loving intimacy.

inspired by Psalm 89

Eternity

You have been our sheltering place
through every generation.
Your love reaches back
beyond the formation of the world.

As children of the earth
we all return to the ground.
Time means nothing;
years pass like a night's sleep
or like the flower that lasts a day.

Our span is seventy years,
a bit longer if we are strong.
We think it's hard and lament our lot.
Then like a thread snapping we're gone.

As each day dawns,
renew our balance.
Help us see past sadness
and present joy in perspective.

Let your loveliness be our fight.
Bless all of us, young and old;
and may our daily work
reflect the splendor of your work.

inspired by Psalm 90

Protect Us

We all live in the shelter
created by God.
God is like a great bird that gathers us
under her wing.

If we are trapped, God frees us.
If we are sick, God heals us.

If we are afraid, God strengthens us.
If we are threatened, God protects us.

God's messengers look out for us.
They support us in difficult times.

To know God's name is to walk in confidence.

inspired by Psalm 91

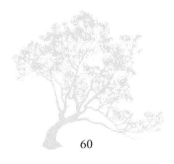

Love and Justice

It is good
to be able to show our gratitude to God.
At dawn and at dusk
we turn to you in praise.

I am in awe at what you accomplish.
It is sad to see that many
are unaware of your graciousness.

The good oil of your love
strengthens me.
Tall trees remind me of your faithful servants.
Old fruit trees remind me of so many of your people
who go on giving themselves
throughout their lives.

We cannot fault God's love and justice.

inspired by Psalm 92

Holiness

When I gaze on the mountains
wreathed in mist,
I see your glory.

When I stand on the cliffs
and watch the ocean's fury,
I see your strength.

Yet you are above beauty,
above strength;
holiness is the mark of your presence.

inspired by Psalm 93

Arrogance

Arrogance is the opposite of godliness.
It is disturbing to see
the arrogance of many people.
They are responsible
for many of the evils
that beset the community of nations.

God sees and hears;
God knows all empty thoughts.

We take heed of the Lord's teaching.
Against the threat of evildoers,
we call on your strength.
When we slip,
your love supports us.
When we are burdened,
you lift the weight from our spirits.

inspired by Psalm 94

God Is Great

Come! Let us sing of our joy.
Acknowledge the presence of God with praise.
God is great; the foundations of the earth attest it.
God is great; the oceans proclaim it.
All creation is God's handiwork.

There have been times when we have not listened
    to God.
In our desert times we grumble and turn away.
Though we had evidence of God's goodness,
we wouldn't accept it.
We had to learn that until we accepted
God as our guide,
we would wander without direction.

inspired by Psalm 95

God's Goodness

Every day calls for a new song of gratefulness to God.
We have seen the falseness of our own idols.
Let us tell the world what we have discovered.

God's rule is just.
God's holiness fills the earth.
Look around, all creation sings of God's goodness.
God brings harmony to the earth.

inspired by Psalm 96

God's Light

The earth proclaims God's potency
in mighty signs:
clouds speak of presence;
fire cannot be resisted;
lightning provides insight;
erosion points to the frailty of even the strongest.

If we can read the signs,
God's light will fall on us,
bringing joy and faithfulness.

inspired by Psalm 97

God's Potency

God's potency shines out in wonderful deeds.

When nations act justly,
when we witness merciful love,
when we see loyalty practiced,
then even the earth joins in the hymns of praise.

inspired by Psalm 98

Prayer of Gratitude

Join the procession to honor God.

Be glad and joyful.

Enter your sacred space with thankfulness.

Let your prayer be one of gratitude for God's love.

inspired by Psalm 100

Remember Us

This is my prayer, listening God.
Answer me at once.
This is my hour of need.
My life is passing like smoke on the horizon.
My heart withers like grass in summer's heat.
I am too sad to think of food.

Like a seagull stranded inshore,
like an owl haunting old ruins,
I sit mantled in loneliness.

You, Lord, are remembered in every age.
Remember us as we cling to the rubble
of our narrow visions.
Hear us;
we were created to acknowledge your goodness.
We are keeping a record of your gifts.
You listen to the homeless;
you hear the prisoner's groan.

God, I am broken in my prime.
My days are limited.
I envy your everlastingness as I contemplate
    my decay.
I know that mountains, too, will crumble.
Like favorite clothes,
everything wears out.
You, our God, will always be the same.

inspired by Psalm 102

God's Love Endures

This is a litany of the gifts of God.

God forgives sin and heals brokenness.
God colors our lives and gives us the strength
    of eagles.
God is just and defends hopeless cases.
God teaches us how to live godly lives.

God is tender and caring.
God doesn't get angry as we do.
God doesn't treat us with contempt.
East or west, God's forgiveness stretches to all.

God's love endures even if we don't.
Like fragile flowers caught by a gust of wind,
the place where we were will be empty.

God's love has lasted through all ages.
Bless the Lord, messengers of God.
Bless the Lord, creatures of God.
And special blessings from me.

inspired by Psalm 103

In Praise of Creation

God, your presence fills the earth.
You are dressed in radiance.
Your creative genius is hard to comprehend.

Look at the ocean: it seems limitless.
A whole world lives within,
creatures strange and familiar.
The mighty whale is like a toy in the bath to you.
Across the surface of the deep
our ships go to and fro like leaves on the tide.
All in the sea world look to you for food.
You hold out your hand and they feast from it.
Your breath is life.

Let God continue to delight in creating.
A look from God and the earth quivers,
one pat and the mountain erupts.

I will sing the song of praise of creation.
As long as I live, let my song give joy to God.

inspired by Psalm 104

Stories of God

Sing and dance in your search for God.
Look everywhere and drink in the divine presence.
You are called to tell the stories of God.

Know the ancient stories of God's presence
     among us;
these were recorded by grateful people.
They believed that God asked loyalty from them.
They acknowledged that everything they had came
     from God.

Even when they were still a wandering tribe,
they felt God's protective presence.
In the times of hunger,
they remembered the great famine.
When the staff of life was broken,
they remembered the gift of Joseph,
a man mistreated, who became their savior.

We, too, must continue the line of storytellers.

inspired by Psalm 105

Sing and Rejoice

Praise God! God of everlasting love!

Here are more deeds of God.
Happy are those who keep God's law and act
    with justice.

We are sinners but you share salvation with us.
Our ancestors sinned, too.
While in Egypt they ignored your signs.
Though they rebelled at the Red Sea, you
    saved them.

God heeded their plight,
their cries of distress,
because of the covenant.
God loved the people with a parent's love.
Their captors witnessed this love.

The people of Israel recorded God's mighty deeds.
They taught us to sing and rejoice in thankfulness.

inspired by Psalm 106

The Way of the Wise

With my whole heart I join the just
in singing God's praise.
Who can forget what God has done?
God, merciful and kind, gives us nourishment.

Faithful God guides us in just paths.
Holy God calls us to a covenant relationship.

With wisdom we learn a reverential fear and awe.
This is the way of the wise: they praise God forever.

inspired by Psalm 111

Parents and Children

Parents who love God
and delight in God's leadership
will have children who are truly blessed.
They will grow strong and true.

Their households will thrive with integrity.
The light of God's mercy and justice
will banish the darkness of fear.
They will lend generously
and deal fairly with others.
They will support the poor.

Bad news will not destroy them.
They know that hatred and revenge are destructive.

inspired by Psalm 112

Heart at Rest

I am filled with love because the Lord hears me.
Death gripped me like the teeth of a trap.
Grief held me in strong bonds;
I cried out to be rescued.

Kind and gentle God, you raised me.
My heart is at rest: safe in God's love.
God wiped my eyes
and steadied my feet.
I walk with confidence.

What gift do I give God?
I raise a toast with the cup of freedom.
When I pray, I call myself "child" and "your servant."
My gift is thankfulness.

inspired by Psalm 116

The Gate of Justice

Because you have saved me,
I journey to you.

The gate of justice is open to all
who love right living.
Even stones rejected by builders have a place.
In God's work a poor stone can support a corner.
Blest are all who come doing God's work.

Let us all make of ourselves
a place of peace and light.

God's love is forever.

inspired by Psalm 118

Cherish the Word

Happy are those who seek God wholeheartedly;
they cherish the way of goodness.
God's way is their way.

How do the young stay single-minded?
By cherishing the word of God.
The way of God is a treasured pathway.

Show me your kindness, God.
Against evil influences
I cling to your law.
Your word is my constant guide.
Help me to live your truth.
Suffering has been my teacher.
I am learning humility.

Your word is a lamp,
a light on my way.
I have pledged to be on the side of justice.
Neither fear nor human judgment will ensnare me.
Keep me thirsty for your truth.
Let your encouragement lead me on.
I will be faithful to your name.

inspired by Psalm 119

True Peace

I look to the mountains,
but they cannot help me.
The creator of the mountains and the plains
is my guide and my help.

God does not sleep,
so is ever watchful of me.
Even the forces of nature cannot harm my soul.
True peace keeps me secure.

inspired by Psalm 121

The House of God

I heard the call to enter God's presence.
In the house of God there is perfect unity.

All people are welcome;
there are no distinctions.
The only law
is to honor the name of God.

Our prayer is for an honorable peace,
for happiness in every home
for the safety of all.

This is the meaning of "Peace be with you."
Our prayer is for the building up of all.

inspired by Psalm 122

Attentiveness

My eye is attentive
to the movement of God,
just as an apprentice is attentive
to the actions of the expert.

I have been wounded
by the sneers and scorn of others.

Let me focus only on your great kindness.

inspired by Psalm 123

The Architect of Our Plans

If God is not the architect of our plans,
then they are doomed to failure.
How foolish to think
that early risings
and late nights
will accomplish the work of God.

Those who please God
are blessed even as they sleep.

Children are a blessing from God.
They bring blessings to their parents
and all who care for them.

There is a special energy
in the children born of young parents.

inspired by Psalm 127

Reverence

Reverence for God is right.
It will lead you along God's path.

Your table will show the bounty of God
and the work of your hands.

Warmth, fruitfulness,
and companionship
will envelop you.

The next generation will be like
new shoots in the spring garden.

These are the blessings that flow from reverence.

inspired by Psalm 128

Mercy and Pardon

From the very depths of the pit I cry.
Hear me! Hear me, Lord.

My distress is great.
Let my pleading reach you.

We could not survive
if you remembered
our sins and shortcomings.

Your all-embracing forgiveness
leaves me in awe.

I trust in God, ever faithful,
knowing, like those on night shift,
that dawn will come.

Let us all be faithful watchers.
God's mercy and pardon are ours.

inspired by Psalm 130

Tranquility

I'm not too proud to seek help.

My alms are set according to my talents.

I am calm and tranquil.

I rest secure in the motherly arms of God.

My whole being knows at-one-ness.

inspired by Psalm 131

Aliens

We sat by the river, weeping,
our tears part of the alien stream.
We hung our harps in the trees.

Let the wind provide their music.

Our captors wanted entertainment:
"Sing us your native songs!"

Our native songs are songs of God's goodness.
How can we sing our precious songs
to an unfeeling people?

We will never forget our heritage.
Our anger blazes against our captors.
Let our voices be silent unless we speak of you,
O God, our greatest joy.

inspired by Psalm 137

Circle of Praise

My whole being is a hymn of praise to you, O God.
I acknowledge your presence with me.
Your love and fidelity are seen by all.
When I call for strength, you act.

Around the world comes a circle of praise.
Your people sing of your ways.
You attend to the lowly;
you keep an eye on the haughty.

If I have to face difficulties, you are my support.
The promise of your strength saves me.

Your love lasts forever.
Do not abandon your own creation.

inspired by Psalm 138

You Are There

Lord, you know me thoroughly;
you are aware of whatever I'm doing.
If I'm walking or at rest,
you know where I've been.
When I'm preparing to speak,
you know what I'm going to say.
I feel this as a pressure;
it's beyond my understanding.

Is it possible to hide from you?
Is your presence really all-encompassing?

I climb mountains, you are there.
I dive into the ocean, you are there.
I fly into the dawn, you are there.
I travel to remote islands, you are there.
I draw night around me but this is no disguise.
I am your handwork.
The knitting cast on in my mother's womb,
my form taking shape in secret.
You watched my body grow according to
     your design.

Your thoughts are many and include all creation:
the sands on all the shores cannot compare.
They are beyond my imagining.

I profess to be on the side of justice and right.
Search my heart, lest I wander from your ways.

inspired by Psalm 139

Like Incense

Hurry, Lord, hurry!
I plead with you.
Let my prayer rise like incense.

Lord, place a guard on my lips,
so that my words are well considered.
Keep me from the extravagances of evil.

If the just admonish me,
let me ponder their judgment.
If I am slandered,
let me stand firm,
trusting in your wisdom.

In you, Lord, I find my safety.
Do not let me be prey to the unexpected.

inspired by Psalm 141

My Companion

Hear me, faithful Lord!
Bend to me with compassionate love.
Treat me with tenderness,
for no one is sinless in your sight.

I feel hunted and caged by alien forces.
My strength fails and my soul is dry.

Show me your presence;
I feel the breath of the grave.
Let each new dawn announce your love,
for my hope is in you.

I make a morning offering of myself.
Teach me your will for me.
Gracious Lord, be my companion,
for I belong to you.

inspired by Psalm 143

A New Song

I'll sing to the Rock
who prepares me for life.
Like a mountain fastness, you protect me.

Why do you care for us?
Why concern yourself with us
when our lives are so brief?
You snatch us from the raging seas
of our own disturbance.
You rescue us from the lies of strangers.

I'll sing a new song,
with the instrument of my life
in the company of all the saints
who have praised your name.

inspired by Psalm 144

God's Visible Love

Let my whole life be a song of praise.
I do not place my trust in worldly wisdom.
Its span is short, crumbling into dust.

The wise look to God, Creator.
God's covenant love is visible.
The hungry are fed.
The poor receive justice.
The captives are set free.
The blind receive new sight.
The bent and twisted experience strength.
The bereaved are comforted.
The stranger finds a protector.

The kingdom of God endures forever.
It takes root in every generation.
Hallelujah!

inspired by Psalm 146

The Peace of God

How lovely the sound of the praise of God!
God builds up the shattered.
God gathers the exiles, mending broken hearts.

Look at the stars.
God knows their names.
Great is our God beyond all telling.
Give thanks to God with full voice.

The rain that greens the hills is a gift from God.
God feeds the birds and the various animals.
If they have strength and endurance,
it is a gift from God.

Where God is acknowledged is a holy place.
We seek the peace of God in our lands.

God speaks to the earth through daily reflections.
Snow, hail, frost, and cold reveal God at work.
When the spring thaw comes,
we again give glory for the breath of God,
sustaining and renewing
in desert dryness or tropical lushness.

God's gift is bestowed freely.

inspired by Psalm 147

Sing Praise

Creation sings thanksgiving to God.
Messengers of God, sing praise.
Sun and moon, twinkling stars, sing praise.
Rain clouds, tidal pools, sing praise.

Mountain peaks and ocean depths, sing praise.
Gales and breezes, sing praise.
Moss and fern and fruiting trees, sing praise.
Dogs, cats, sheep, and cattle, sing praise.
Untamed animals, sing praise.
Birds of every hue, sing praise.
Reptiles and insects large and small, sing praise.

Leaders of people, sing praise.
Those who serve others, sing praise.
Women and men, sing praise.
The very old and the newly born, sing praise.
Those who are suffering, sing praise.

God's splendor colors the earth.
God's glory shines out in faithful people.
Let us all sing praise.

inspired by Psalm 148

New Songs

Let there be new songs
from faithful people.
With instruments and dance
recall God's name.

The Lord delights in helping us.
Start the song with full voice.
Let it swell from clan to clan,
nation to nation.

Those who cannot rejoice will be challenged.
May their hearts be moved by the joy of the faithful.

inspired by Psalm 149

Praise God

Praise God in holy places.
Praise the mighty deeds of God.

Praise God, all players of musical instruments
in orchestras, quartets, bands, or as soloists.

All that is alive, praise God!

inspired by Psalm 150

First Servant Song

Look!
Here is my disciple.

I chose him.
He bears my spirit.

He will do no damage.
No one will be hurt by him,
not even the most fragile.

Delicate flower and tender shoot
will flourish in his presence.

This is the way of peace—
my way.

Take this message to everyone.

inspired by Isaiah 42

Second Servant Song

Pay attention!

God's spirit has been with me from my beginning.

I am a finely honed instrument,
but God keeps me under wraps.

I am skilled in the cut and thrust of debate,
but God asks for silence.

I have been a constant worker,
but I have nothing to show for it.

I am disciple—
the lantern, not the light.

inspired by Isaiah 49

100

Third Servant Song

My eloquence comes from God.
My gift is for the weary,
so that I may offer words of consolation,
words that will lift them up.

Each morning God calls me to listen,
even to those who are silent.
I could have rebelled,
but I did not turn my back on them.
I have been humiliated by taunts,
but God has helped me bear the pain.

When I am challenged, God walks beside me.
God is my help,
even though I may be judged by human standards.

inspired by Isaiah 50

101

Fourth Servant Song

My servant will grow in strength.
He may look beaten and cowed,
but you will be astonished.
You will all stand speechless.

The story is for everyone.
This wretched one was once beautiful.
Like a blade of grass in desert places,
he grew in grace.

Now there is no outward bearing to attract our eyes.
Like an outcast, he is avoided.
He is marked by suffering and degradation.
We did not recognize that it was our shadow that
    he bore.

We gazed at him and did not see ourselves.
Because he did not turn from his suffering,
his light will shine for many,
bringing wholeness and reconciliation.

inspired by Isaiah 52 and 53

102

I Am One Who Knows Affliction

God has called me to walk in darkness,
not in the light.
I am fenced in by my poverty and weariness.
I dwell in the dark like one long dead.

My soul knows no peace.
I have forgotten what happiness is;
I tell myself that I have no future.
Reflecting on my helplessness leaves me distraught.
What can I do to give me a reason to hope;
to believe that the forces of good are not exhausted?

The grace of God is renewed for me each morning,
so great is God's faithfulness.
It is good to wait in silence for the saving help
    of God.

God does not rejoice in our pains
but watches out for those who suffer.
God is not unconcerned.
Why, then, do I feel so inconsolable?
Why do I weep without comfort?

I call to you, God, from the bottom of the pit,
even as the waters of death rise over me.
You, Lord, are my strength.
You call to me, "Fear not!"

inspired by Lamentations 3

The Word of God
Is like Mother Wisdom

Mother-like, she will meet you;
like a spouse, she will embrace you.

Wisdom will nourish you with the bread of
   understanding
and give you the water of learning to drink.

You will lean on her and not fall,
you will trust in her and not feel shame.

You will feel strong and confident
and be eloquent when you speak of her.

Joy and gladness will be your companions.

In the beginning when you were created,
God shared with you the ability to make choices.

Each day is set before you fire and water;
you can stretch out your hands and choose.

Each day is set before you life and death;
whatever you choose is yours.

inspired by Sirach 15

Holy Wisdom

Before you the whole universe is as a grain on a balance
or a drop of morning dew come down upon the earth.

But you have mercy on all, because you can do
    all things;
and you overlook our sins that we may repent.

For you love all things that are,
and loathe nothing that you have made,

For what you hated, you would not have fashioned.
And how could a thing remain in existence, unless
    you willed it;
or be preserved, had it not been called forth by you?

But you spare all things, because they are yours,
O Lord and lover of souls.

For your imperishable spirit is in all things!

Therefore, you rebuke offenders little by little.
You warn them, and remind them of the sins they are
    committing,
that they may abandon their wickedness and believe
    in you, O Lord!

inspired by Wisdom 11:22–12:2

In Search of Wisdom
and Her Blessings

Happy the one who meditates on wisdom,
and reflects on knowledge.
Who ponders her ways and understands her paths.

Who tracks her like a scout and waylays her at her gate.
Who peeps in at her windows and listens at her doors.

Who camps near her house and lives as a welcome
    neighbor.
Who builds a nest in her tree and makes a home in
    the branches.

Mother-like, she will meet him;
like a young bride, she will embrace him.
Nourish him with the bread of understanding;
give him the water of learning to drink.

He will lean on her and not fall;
he will trust in her and not be embarrassed.

When God created us, we were given the gift of choice.
If you choose, you can follow God's way.
There is set before us fire and water.
Whatever we choose will be given to us.

inspired by Sirach 14:20ff.

A Blessing for All Fathers

Holy be the name of our God.

God of our fathers, their fathers, and all fathers,
stretching back through all generations.

For God has once again visited us
and brought our families out of exile.

We had a sign of saving strength in our ancestor
    David,
a good man and loyal servant.

God has kept his word to us.
A saving word that our brothers, the prophets,
reminded us of time and time again.

From enemies of every kind God saves us,
particularly the threat of crippling fear.

We remember his great mercy to Abraham, Jacob,
and all our tribal leaders,
and the promises he made in solemn treaty.

God freed us for holy service
so that we could spend our days

growing in God's strength,
learning his wholeness.

You, little one, who brings me fatherhood,
will join the noble line of holy men.

Strong, courageous messengers of God,
spiritual pioneers braving the wilderness,
creating the paths for the movement of God among
    his people.

Through you, many will learn that God saves,
that God forgives,
that God loves.

This fathering is truly a great work.
A sign of the kindness of God,
our Day-Spring, who brings us light.

With darkness gone, we can dwell in peace.

inspired by Luke 1:68-79

Come to the Table

All you who thirst, come to the source!

If you have no money, come.
You will receive what you need.

What I offer is free, no strings attached!

You are hungry,
yet you spend money on what cannot satisfy.

Be attentive and you shall eat well.
My table is laden with rich fare.

Listen mindfully;
what I offer is life.

The covenant I made with you long ago stands firm.

When you look for me,
you sometimes look in all the wrong places.
I'm not far away;
I'm beside you.

Put away whatever causes you harm.
Are you afraid that I'll remember your past failings?

I do not act as you act.
I do not dwell on the past.

Think of spring.
Rain falls.
It waters the earth.

The soil regains its fertility.
Wheat grows, flour becomes bread.
Humankind is nourished.

Think of your spiritual springtime.
My word falls on you.
It takes root.

You use the word for your nourishment.
You grow and become strong.

Joy and peace shall be your traveling companions.
As you journey, the mountains and hills will break
    into song;
gorse and brambles will become rosebushes.
The earth will proclaim
the goodness of the Lord.

inspired by Isaiah 55

The Gathering of What
Has Been Scattered

From now on, therefore, we consider no one
from a human point of view;
even though we once considered Christ
from a human point of view,
we judge him thus no longer.

Therefore, if anyone is in Christ,
they are a new creation;
the old order has passed away;
behold, the new has come.

All this has been done by God,
who, through Christ,
reconciled us to the Divine
and gave us the ministry of reconciliation.

I mean that God, in Christ,
was reconciling the world to the Divine,
not counting their transgressions against them,
and entrusting a message of reconciliation to us.

This makes us ambassadors for Christ,
God making this appeal through us.
We beseech you in Christ's name,
be one with God.

inspired by 2 Corinthians 5:16-20

Listen to God as God Speaks to You

I created you;
I formed you from the stuff of the universe.

Do not be afraid.
I have given you your name, precious beautiful one.

When you experience fear, I am there.
When you feel as if you're drowning, I will hold you up.
When you burn with confusion and doubt yourself,
    I will stay with you.

I am holy, whole;
you are becoming holy, whole, healed.

Because you are precious in my eyes, glorious,
and because I love you,
I would exchange the riches of the earth for you.

You may feel scattered but I will make you whole.
Do not dwell too long on old pains.
Let me do something new in you.

Look! See, a new way springs up before you.

inspired by Isaiah 43

Forgiveness

If anyone has given offense,
she has hurt not only me,
but in some measure all of you.

You should now forgive and support her,
so that she may not be crushed
by too great a weight of sorrow.

I beg you to reaffirm your love for her.

I thank God who unfailingly leads us on
in Christ's rejoicing company
and uses us to spread the perfume
of Christ's knowledge everywhere!

We are the perfume of Christ for God's sake!

We speak in Christ's name,
pure in motivation,
conscious of having been sent by God
and of being ever in God's presence.

inspired by 2 Corinthians 2